Para,Taxis

Para,Taxis

Greg Darms

Radiolarian Press · Astoria, Oregon · 2010

Radiolarian Press
92673 John Day River Road
Astoria, OR 97103

First Edition

ISBN 978-1-887853-30-9

Katagami: Web of Butterflies and Flowers has appeared
(in Russian translation) in *Apraksin Blues.*

Cape D Light has been exhibited in Astoria as part of an art work
of the same title incorporating text and graphite drawing.

Cover Art by Greg Darms from *Continuum of Difference*

I think the Heart I former wore
Could widen –

contents

ten poems

Study for Self-Portrait

given this   before falling
               half reflected
catching
light's limit
               one eye
standing   for itself

recollecting
seeing, seen   this
               is memory

the left side   lit in glass
the right   the way
               eyes see
twice,
               once
from each   perspective

and once   from both

who I was
               I am

Mudstone, Stiff Boom, Hard Ground

A form shaped from native clay
dug from red-orange ochre grit-mud,
slippery, yielding little to the digging hand.

The elements known in terms of the elements,
lag bolts drilled through pressure-treated boards
sistered vertically and sunk in sound fir stringers.

This reality, itself, potent as a rock.
Bones, the hard ground, inside and out at once –
an art like steel, forged, untarnished within.

Katagami: Web of Butterflies and Flowers

Summer rain – permeating
the roots of all things
in the underground solution of earth,
founding the material universe.

Summer rain – running off
bare leaves, bare arms,
as if involved in a tryst
with the three cool elements.

Summer rain – lingering
petunias fade with the season.
The new geese are gone,
having learned to fly.

Turning to the question of today's work –
how many impressions can be made
from a breakable thing?

Daily Conceit

Something involving squares,
Four, nine, sixteen of them,
how they were assembled.
backlit utterances
monofilament, crumpled papers,
window. Tangy stuff
Splintered, shocked,
little narratives
applied to the surface
pulled out and pinned to the wall.
to keep from breaking or burning.
a fine line, a wet image

that kind of memory.
what they were made of,
Nervous exposures,
equidistant from a point,
lead-weighted rope, broken
is the matter.
quadrilateral, unpaginated,
dredged, netted, hooked,
of what remains,
Crying or laughing
Something taking shape,
resolved to enter the day.

Svensen Farm

New lit wings inscribe slightly downward arcs.
Small red volumes ascend in spiral segments.
A gust explodes from some concept of egg.
The lawn is punctuated with self-heal and daisy.
Violet-greens work to fill a parcel of sky.
A black and red ant touches a thousand things.
Equal in tone and duration, six peeps declare.
Dead and dull things are left hanging from plants.
A sparrow's cadence is a surprising identity.
I find this spring day I have done this before.
The disconnected flight and drift are joined.
By four senses I concur with the general agitation.
Surfaces become complex, more yellow.
Terrestrial, we feel the sun for a change.

By Word and By Deed

Coming to rely on what the day offers –
the weather, the state of my bones,
restless geese over the switching yard –

turning against the grain of traffic
I pull up to a full stop
by a razor wire fence.

I ignore the warnings.
I am not trespassing where
I own the words, where I walk

as I will, leaving marks of graphite
below my feet as fierce dark proof.

Shadow of What Was Seen

butt end of windfall hemlock
smooth rock where it meets the river
the afternoon understory

using available pigments I moved
from point to point with
changing eyes, I tried it
from here and from here,
gave it a sense of relief,
followed myself in the hand

darker, wet green alders
last season's detrital subfloor
contour of forest or heaven

Annunciation (Skokomish Wilderness)

Rain shadow sun on wet stinging nettles
fractured, both fractured

River words in the understory dazzle
mistaken for language

Minim of red, vine maple seed, dove, vole
clearing the vision

Large cat tracks (no claws) in the dust, in the road
empty of content

Spider threads from some other sky
beg for notice

Hint of something like luck, faint thunder
doe with child

Sudden cool down-valley breeze, something
that is shadow itself

Cape D Light

when that is all I really want to see

all there is time for, then

when it reaches, looking up, the sky

where it curves around and behind the surface

when an urge to see the other side wins

the light is such it dazzles

when more than contour is apparent

and matters of form take over

and are taken over by shadows

and I see myself in it

Moment of Stasis

The twelve minutes between tides, on the river.

Wherever the wind stops, the traffic disappears.

The distances sound close as the air on your face.

Mercury comes out of retrograde, the moon is full.

The top of the planet looks down on every latitude.

Spinning around the center, eyeing the storm.

Each extreme reach of the pendulum's arc.

The zenith of the archer's unstrung quill.

The nulling dark and death of a momentary blink.

The stopped second hand every second's tick.

One humming heartbeat, wingbeat, breath.

The instant flare of meteor, eye's after-flare.

The number one, the number no one counts.

The dying breath following the last of words.

The leaf or nebula seen with a raptor's eye.

The falcon's stoop stopped just before the kill.

Any day of this life I find myself alive –

Foolish Parmenides thinking this will always be.

on the knowable

composed using vocabulary selected from Herbert Spencer's
First Principles (1900)

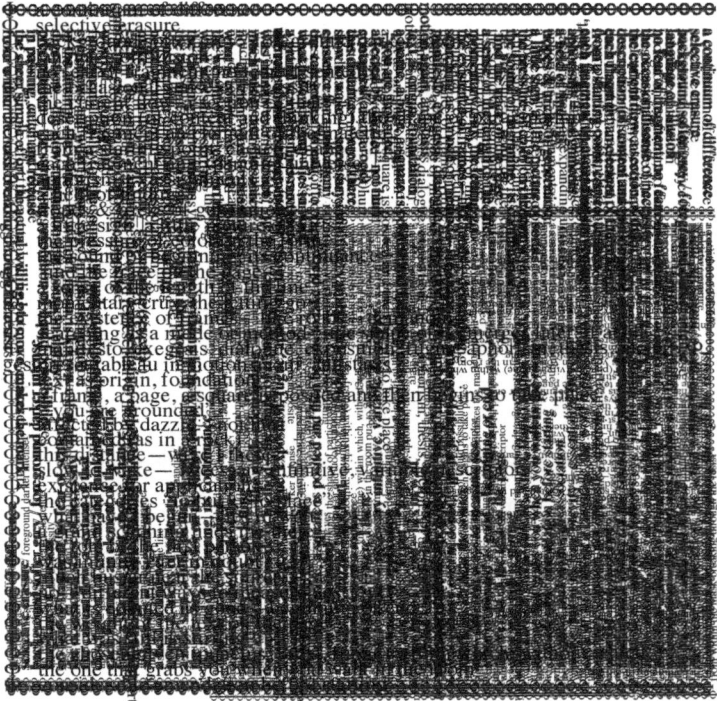

selective erasure

the one that grabs you

so that it reflected the actual things

                                                   especially the mirror

things which appeared

light,
surface

                                            seen in a great mirror

                                     an indistinguishable cloud

the bottom of the waters

continuum
through
the objects

                                       but more often reality

                                           was made
                                           to present
                                              itself

it was not   the expression
of pure reality

                                                                    of form

a new plastic reality

inexorable

once alive we are
concrete
                                        to that end he utilized
                                            the laboratory

mirror

                                         the dark

reflected

                                           a thing

more than an image –

                                           it is

depth in a narrow circle

we have seen

                                        a mistaken

mind

                                        process of

conscious
of nature

                                    the visible screen

a theory

                            a tardy recognition of the
                                                current

of nature

enclosed within
delivered thereby

mutable

                             superficial

eyes

                             divested of
                                 clarity

so closed up

                            beneath the
                  whole surface of the soul

                          entirely feathered

results in a disturbed field

piece of

always for

its own time

little adjustments, minute beginnings from mute endings

truth branches & braids, twines & diverges, splits & binds, pauses & leaps
– dendritic, alluvial, corpuscular

incremental, layered, sequential, mixed, elemental, compounded, partial,
scattered, joined & gathered

papers & beads, needles & yarn, glass, glasses, prayers, birth
announcements, commencements, days, images, powder, perfume,
arthritis magnets, numbers & cards, arts & crafts, keepsakes, letters,
my promise, books, funnies, patterns, boxes, buttons, mirrors, pills,
her savior, her mother, her children, blankets, missals, epistles

chalk yellow prism, woodbound stick of pierre noire, deep vermilion,
raw and burnt ochre umber, shadow scum, gesso, resin, nuggets, pebbles,
spondees, & rocks

occurrences of iron, zinc, copper, lead, ceramic, glass, steel, tin, things
elemental in vast plains of loss, things drawn in history beginning to
accrete into strange conglomerates collected by no one, by gravity, as
refuse, as a kind of made (by no one) subject

each day's sentence, a string of findings, castings & foundings, hooks,
snags & catches, night's eaches slipping back and away

science of description, art of science, question of art, truth of question, desire
of truth, universe of desire, beauty of universe, description of beauty

green phyllitic shale shot through with umber-crusted quartz, stalagmitic,
triplanar

tracing, rubbing, impression, after-image residue, print, track, scat, shape
of gesture, sketch in passing, common incipit, coincidental node of
intersection near collision points, shared language moment

the river, my shadow, my hand, the point of focus, something big, the sky, the ground, a figure, a day, the road, the city, a landmark, clouds, the letter *a*

last and first things, space, fields of run and fields of see, brainflicker night-long in flurries and sparks, the quality of a particular, a mystery, stacks of photos, faces, forms, leaves of words, pressed allium, skin tabs, quotes, dimensions of attention, relatives, fruiting bodies

wet fell field, marmot, mourning cloak, split rock, joint, fracture, fault, block, shard, aster, brass button, arnica, buckwheat, penstemon, crevice, pale phacelia, heather, anemone, finch, nutcracker, lichen

forge, illuminate, fold, unravel, mimic, caress, leap, drift, sigh, condense, evaporate, hum, waltz, rest, wake, cut the deck

a century of little gems & massive veins, a collection of aorist gazes, broadsides of such and such, the prima materia & the soul of a saint, a gestural record of the metonymic moment, a serial adventure starring several illustrious pre-Socratics

moving through the square, the idea part of it, thinking ahead stopped
for the next light, walking the line with a stylus, breathing falling light &
learning lost places, finding edges in the space of white silence, living like
nothing in the world moves like empty weeds, grounded in sky & figured
in ground, running with wild symbolic elements, following a thread
through the city between armillary spheres

the moment lit – radiance, luster, flare, foxfire, flash, dazzle

what wonders in the glass & wanders in the mind, opaque fixity & the play
of metamorphoses, edge of yourself impregnated with carbon, lemon of
sulfur, gold, the tension and relaxing of forms

the curve we generate, pausing for something like thought

november fragments

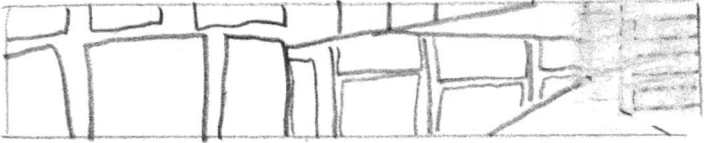

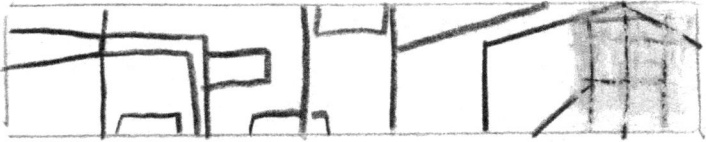

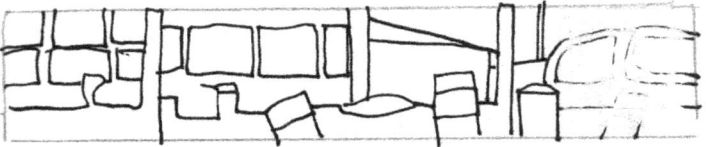

1   What have I thought through the day? What is most near at hand in time, harder to retrieve year after year, is a feeling of mind, rather than a consideration of feeling.

2   To get it is what I am to do, somewhere between a full stop and an ellipsis: make something of the page.

3   I came here to draw, despite the security men with too many eyes and the white noise klaxon. But the towering objects are almost too subjective.

4   An idea: an essay about a description of looking into an idea about process.

5   Most attempts at project descriptions involve a linguistic approximation of the present *en passant,* like a recipe for an ephemera cocktail.

6   One is always first again as well as the ultimate product and quotient.

7   Work of the day: body, mind, and soul, in sitting, walking, and drawing.

8   And music, as in a touch of spice whelms the bland sauce, as in the knowledge attained through food.

9   Sit for once long and still enough to gaze. Forget why you came or thought you had to go, even if you have to force your eyes open to see what lies between. Reports from all provinces indicate the most unexpected beings will visit you in that unmeasured nowhere, and may even sit on your opened hand.

10   Soon enough one starts making things up: it often happens on its own. But the effort to try to see where and how it starts is rewarding in itself, given the universal belief in the existence of the one who makes and sees. Thus thinking makes one visible.

11   About the *line which begins outside the window* the world thinks.

12   Distant, friends' (authors') voices over stacks and shelves, across rooms and decades – an occasional poem noted or book announced, date of reading posted – yet near in the sense of the pulse in the ear.

13   Thinking, thinking – words, words: a project outside in the world, outside that world.

14   Sometimes a big silence from the audience, but look at the eyes, at the muscles in various corners of the face, listen to the growing murmur of the countenance. Some bicameral grunt or cry, sigh, retort or yay waits for a walk on the beach to surface.

15   Returning in the rain, slightly grayer and cast down, the three jobs done for now, a little time suggests itself by a reflection of cloud light on the river, by a feeling in the ears that an orchestra is tuning in the pit.

16   The superimposed architecture of books shelved leaning one way, pencils points up in an old festival glass, telecommunications connectors arcing over each other like freeways, papers on papers and papers bent, folded, and skewed define the planes of desk and wall by gesture and ephemeral form. All or none of these things are necessary for the world to exist.

17   It is not necessary for the world to exist for language to create the world.

18   A thing. A word. A world.

19   A thing is more visibly real when its perimeter is walked in baby steps.

20   One result of the history of tongue and eye and hand is the difference between word and world.

21   Three days of preparation, yet just one look is all it took. There are many ways to get there, twelve gates once you do. Within the given construct as it were.

22   We live once each time a parent dies. *Adequatio.* What a conference call that will be, on the day the ship comes in.

23   The audience, in its variorum of the ear, senses little differences in the larger approach.

24   A project of words, the *ars aura lingua,* is an irresistible old piano.

25   What is heard, or what is seen, is one way in. Handily restated later it is one way to be, reinstated.

26   A number is identical to some other number, yet has nothing to do with it or with the next ordinal except outside of concept or relationship.

27   The next ordinal number, or thing seen, is a question of its own instance.

28   A condition is one result of a chain of chance, of all the little stuff preceding, and a possibility of participating in further concatenation.

29   Once one has entered, or one has realized one has entered, a path – a way – a process – the forgotten incipits, the dead dull days, *lacunae,* and *mals mots* can be equanimitously gathered or dispersed as markers (ascending, descending) of that involved awareness, like Stations of the Cross.

30   Of a day no word was written, this can be said.

december fragments

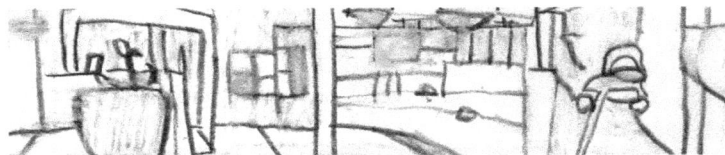

1   What.

2   What state is to the east or west of this (above below, before after, surrounding within)?

3   From eight miles above, county roads on section lines, scattered farm buildings, tiny towns are reminders of insignificance.

4   Conscious of the beauty of (probably unintentional) patterns, structures, designs.

5   White linear fragments partially fill and define the shadow sides of roads, hedgerows, furrows – intaglio compositions within field frames.

6   Reading. Recognition of any number of previously unrecognized lines. Entering one new page after another.

7   Sunset seen from the upper atmosphere, slow sinking comprehension of the less mediated spectrum. In the region of Venus and Jupiter, Prussian blue, cerulean, a band of ochre sienna, finally and ultimately scarlet vermilion – the limit of language, of seeing. Then black Earth.

8   I don't know what kind of tree it is but its form supercedes its being.

9   Whatever was packed will arrive.

10   Revising as far as changing an occasional comma or inflection, and thinking of changing it back.

11   Big turtles sun on a green leaf island, catfish swim in the channel. Either this has the turning which now must be apprehended, or the next set of syllables must carry us on.

12   Sometimes a page contains a week or more, as far as the hand is available. Othertimes a day demands an entire codex.

13   Slow coming to a point of sense of place, a sense of pointing. Morning sun and mist on the Withlacoochie.

14   Millions of gallons a day of clear cool water, anhinga and cormorant resting wings spread, paddling upstream, drifting downstream, weather every day for billions of years.

15   Fortuitous stop, delightful delay – moment of kinesis in stasis.

16   Trains passing each other at 60 thinking "next stop" thinking "destination" – an *idée fixe* at full throttle – moment of stasis in kinesis.

17   Descriptive settings closer to fiction the more accurate, to poetry the more precise, to philosophy the larger the view.

18   How is it determined, the beginning and end of a given (or made) fragment?

19   What (kind of) drawing would illustrate the nightbook? This is an illustrative question.

20   Locations among dis-locations – the multi-body antigravity problem – an infinitude of drawings.

21   Two projects: one drawing of many lines; many drawings of one line.

22   This time no wire to plug in, no source except that exists or is invented in the eye.

23   Some fragments of time, some out of . . .

24   Point to point in a multitude. Call it what the imperative allows – a series of lit arches underground, trains in many directions rumbling farther below.

25   Far afield is near a center.

26   Process: young people move into an old neighborhood, the buildings change from the inside out.

27   Self-knowledge not equivalent to identity.

28   The experience that some books exist but are not to be found.

29   Partial, particulate, possibly later drawing together, drawing out, tracing the perimeter, limning the shape of the walk.

30   How much perspective, in passing through, can you remember – is this one point where imagination might approximate reality?

31   Project: stop on the track (in your tracks), click you know where you are. This often involves looking up or down.

32   What other revelations stirred by this of sight – caught by surprise.

33   Project: prospect, vision, prospectus, manifesto, notion, schema, scenario, conceptualization, invention, musing, construction, cloudcuckooland, structure, frame, figuration, shape, arrangement, matrix, contour, configuration.

34   Start with what I think I am. What=when=where. Desiring: the lost, the absent, the not yet.

35   What part of this peek-a-boo don't I get?

36   This season just past, fall, was a fall – an arc marked by points in an orbit. The arc seen from a different place or time has been drawn, is to be drawn.

37   This=that: drawing anything but conclusion. Based on each breath (step, idea), facing, entering, so as to have been, have being, be.

38   Acceptance of time, that it is real, that it is imaginary.

39   One day lines written, one day lines drawn.

40   The visual in (or from) the words, the idea in (or from) the marks on a surface.

41   Contour, gesture, shape, volume, depth, proportion, perspective (all singular, all plural) in writing as well as in drawing. Concept, incipit, structure, composition, development, closure also seen in each process.

42   Conversely, there is the negative of each verb and noun, but it is not just not "not".

43   What is the negative of *gesture*?

44   Is the negative not isn't the positive?

46   Is what?

in nevada

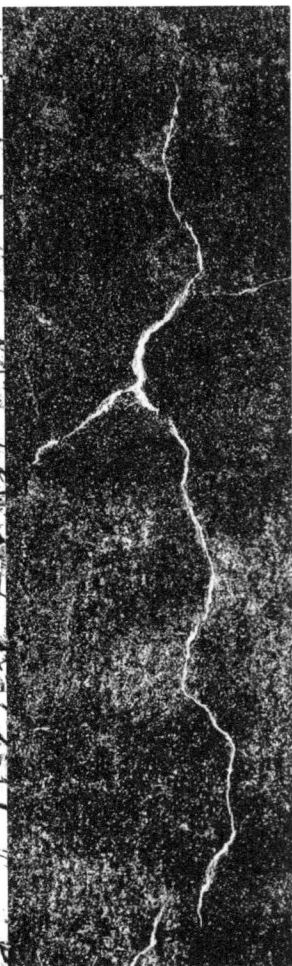

another first attempt at capturing
the moment, what

would it look like something

now the light is deeper,
but I'm losing it

                    infinite perseverance

seventh degree blast of winter
blackbirds cling to cottonwood
absence clings to landforms

long dry Lake Winnemucca –

a methodological field
a process of demonstration
a certain experience of limits
a passage, an overcrossing

playa dust, cold north wind
all night, ice on the glass by morning

broken, can be broken

shadow on dry lake
reverse mirage

one hundred miles good dirt road
a difficult dimension

Hallelujah Junction
HEADLIGHTS ON NEXT 88 MILES

known in part, as part
            of what
was never on a list

approaching what can only be
the end of things, caught
        in the what was
made by always looking back

this big fake solidity,
outside of which some
insubstantial evidence

thirty-five proverbs

translations from *152 proverbes mis au goût du jour*
by Paul Eluard and Benjamin Péret, first published in
La Révolution Surréaliste, Paris, 1925

Before the flood, disarm the brains.

One mattress deserves another.

Don't burn perfumes in flowers.

Elephants are contagious.

It is necessary to return to straw that which concerns girders.

Style is another punishment.

Like an oyster which has found a pearl.

No one rows in the forest.

"Look at my situation," say the heroes to the heroine.

Labyrinths aren't made for dogs.

To wash the tree.

The sun doesn't shine for someone.

Spare the manna, spoil the child.

A bit more green and less blond.

Who doesn't hear me hears everything.

Too many bombs hurt the corn.

The sheet of paper precedes the wind.

Cherries fall where texts missed.

Joyous in the water, pale in the mirror.

To each day its tent is enough.

All that grows huge is not soft.

There is always a pearl in your mouth.

Don't throw away any demons except angels.

You've read everything but drunk nothing.

All which comes to my kitchen grows in my heart.

Always stretch before crawling.

To play violin on Tuesday.

The scholars who are approaching throw their clothes in the ditch.

To get two hours from a clock.

Dance all day or lose your glasses.

Deaf as an ear in a bell.

My neighbor is yesterday or tomorrow.

To crush two cobblestones with the same button.

Be large before being fat.

Life of errors and perfumes.

aurora

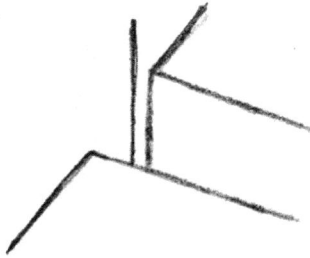

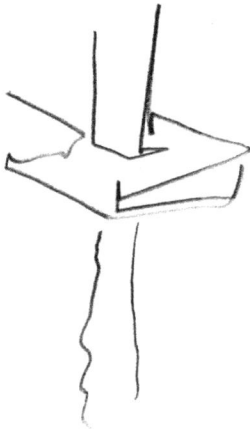

aurora. Passing through the 99 tunnel behind a loaded revolving orange-barrel rocket cement truck, dark glasses bringing on melancholy of apocalypse. Out into the sun of viaduct. Engine noise invisible in the sky. Buses here can only follow the overhead tram lines. Near incidents at every turn. Stadia wait. *I confess I love the surface.* Metal spinning second generation. Need parallel time to go into the environment. Moments of stasis underground where words congeal. One poem prayer is enough. Some of them are under glass. Providing reflections. Often neatly framed, geometrical. Then a quality of light between buildings.

28th NW. Rhododendrons on the north side begin to bloom. What is logic. Echo of virga over the western sound. What is available we are asked to sample. Book of the Sistine Chapel on the morning table. Watch a mote settle. Inner pages unremarked. Inside the glass table lit chestnut spines and cone shadow. Rearrangement. From which corner of the sky. Any number of words preceding which could follow. Proceed. A noun of determinate status. Theory has little or nothing. Can I come in. Who's there. Identification of the early saxifrage as a name forgotten. Repetitive bird call. A wind begins to blow from room to room. Hint of occasional train.

15 South. Cut through my breathing space. Everyone is going faster. Still you are breaking the speed limit. Arc of the thrown rock that will break it seen head on. Weigh in motion. Symbol of our national aggression flying above Barbecue Inn. Gravelly Lake. Black Lake. Replaced by something much faster. Turn west, clouds in my mind. Extra smalls for lunch in a sleepy town. A quiet articulation. High tides make short rivers lakelike. The sedges darker. Stacks of dirt, roots, brush, for some future burn. Finally the bridge to mile zero. Which way you look at it. Do I remember the mysterious nocturnal dancers on the new cement patio. No. At home signs of recent rain.

Rain. Expanding circumferences interfere and dissipate. Making it up each time, making up for lost numbers. Somewhere it accumulates. Patter on both sides of the apex. Runoff, rundown, interstitial processes of swell. One hundred percent chance. Royal history, coronations of splash. Slants and verticals. Segments, one end of each lost in origin. Presentiment of slump and slide. Certain podecipediforms show no sign. Suspension of orange oxides. Once again a reminder of no break in time out there. Is what we call it. Choice of gear for venturing out. A fraction would dissolve these words. It delivers a different kind of light.

Mirror. Hung as rhombus over a small abyss. Long receding view of ceiling looking lit where no light should be. Leaving afterimages on the page of words. Can a shadow fall there, originate there. As in a church full of pious believers chanting in unison. Stranger than which, fact or fiction? Risky end mark. Paths some of which lead in the direction of the heartland. How this language might translate. Today or yesterday when shopping. Summer approaches with its commencements and ripenings. It occurs that this is the time of day when I was born. And what happened to yesterday. At the end of the glassy void another window with its blue complement contained.

What. Fading before lights out, asking, stretching toward the horizontal. One measure of moment, of certainty, by self like gnomon compared to thumb. Quick, it's gone like all the others. High heater whine. Some are seeing pinks and yellows by the road. Watch and glass by the bed. Sometimes lines help. On which to rest or run. Sugars are burned, leaves "flesh" out. A sense of walls within which. Once having seen or otherwise sensed that kind of impossibility. Restless search. Long thin canvas. Night is the time of day. Something surrounding an empty or unknown center. Arcs and tangents. Then power off and it begins.

Routine. Time of, and time of. Rise and shine, fade. Way to work memorized. How many curves this incarnation. Each way few choices. Is it a lie. Yet enough uncertainty to allow the names of the days to sink. Do you want to segue. Is there an accent in that. Just under ten inches for the month. Now ending. A thousand titles for each of a thousand instances. Refraction and interference are responsible. Who am I overlooking these questions. The possible present tense. I am in *a whole galaxy of emptiness* which is in a gallery of universes: primum, mobile, sphere of fixed stars. Another way to cross-multiply and determine the present proportion.

Cormorants. Having descended with rain to the common surface they dive individually. Each with a splash of silver. A further definition of black and light. A general formation, floating, their heads held up at the characteristic angle. What, how, looking, seeing. An intermittent phenomenon as far as we can tell. Low flight touches mercury. A numbers game through the window. Arc and segment follow rules of river. Moments of waiting for turns. Sentient beings seem calm but have mixed feelings. Glass is used in windows and mirrors. Eyes of warm blood in our world. Always at sea level a certain philosophy. At this time of day, some things seen and felt.

Sidewalk. On which fragments of memory (retrieval, storage) lie in pieces. Fading serenely. Individual deaths in headlines. Homeless eyes, but smiling. What was forgotten that was going to be written. A black, then a white, stretch limo. The smells of used books. Manuscript found behind a backroom shelf. An air of expectancy diminished to a point of balance. Or exalted. Very little of what "should have been," very much of everything else. Which angle of looking askance is recommended. Pattern on a tapestry. A particular design executed with flair. Composition of handwritten, wood-cut, and metal-cut elements. Dry mount of a carefully pressed specimen.

Aria. Echo and trill, sound with rhythm what we feel. With words no matter, which is more important. Mounting the continuum with voice. He sits outside the lonely house. She muses on what the words have wrought for the world in its separateness will be changed, is affected. Sometimes a mad scene. Direct by vibration and timbre, titinnabulation and tonality. What is carried and what is delivered. What is received across the threshold. Beyond technique and style, the faithful in chains. Restless twining, reaching for light. Bel canto coloratura, clarity. We come to be pierced by that. The auditorium is still, huge, expectant. We see each other.

Spare. A break as any awareness of moment. In another country (room) walnuts on the table. Six empty easy chairs. Ball-peen hammer and pliers for the nuts. Everything in its place of disarray. In elevated or emerged context, precisely so. Hum of copier on standby. Efforts of professional hands towards material task. A drink of cold water. Underlined phrases in "a brilliant history." Words at hand. Discussion of future numbers. Conditions of interval. Today for example we deal with the advancement of clock time. Funny in all its meanings the general consensus, subsequent acceptance. Is there self-recognition. Falling on a wet grassy slope during the earthquake drill.

Thought. In one sense the past in another current construct. An almost imaginable matrix of nexuses not unlike the library of Alexandria. Gone without a trace. Maybe 200,000 scrolls burned in transit to Cleopatra. An adventurer may follow any thread, look back, get lost, *transmit forms of knowledge in which the knower himself is revealed.* In another sense finding is prime. One must resort to using the available to describe the awakened. This is full. No one said it would be easy. There was a lighthouse there, too. No easy analogy, that. The seven wonders of each instance. Mind, now. In glyphs and cuneiform runes the sum or the parts. Old, old synecdoche.

Friday. Mind unravels with muscles and the day tends toward loss. The evening an unknown. Wind shifts from the north. There are ungathered documents and quotes without ascription. See the first swallow at 6:45. Nice to be that exact. A moment is revealed when something. What was going to be available. Shadows of solids melt. A giant expulsion. Rinsing the scalp. Some old objects are sent to an island in a lake. A wail, laugh, or song. But brief. What is moving, what staying still. Winding down. There is a statement of authority on a given level. "I avoid the first person." What kind of clouds would say such a thing, building upon a truly bold incipit.

Ebb. Sometimes earlier in the life it turned. Someone was there to see and did or didn't. It flowed under a bridge; they walked over. Hard to tell by the surface. Enough spectrum there to absorb or reflect on. Allow the extra second. A section of atmosphere flares. What does it hold in the way of narrative. One looks at one or two are talking. There is a name for any part of this. Later the transcription if a certain quality of luck. Talking on wheels. A shout of sometimes joy. Crested whatever. Maybe the last g-word diving. A general emptying, specific submergence. Who are the characters and how, and why, and what. The drawing surface is agreeably white and toothy.

Plentitude. In which finding a feeling of loss. Beats me. Books gathered again, family reunion. Sixty-something submissions to be sent. They read themselves. Wish otherwise. Writing past point of recovery. Not yet initiation. Pencils of all hardnesses. The way things are. Is a life's work. Which have not been read, which have. Read again. Stunning the word on the page turned to. Because who knows. The history of, the art of. Reconciliation with what is distant. How late is it. *A one and a many.* Twos, threes, and fours. Boxed sets, fascicles. A single unused Chinese wish paper. Bless the codex. Until taken from the shelf and opened.

Retreat. Self-contained sense of opening, as long as it takes. There are games and there is playing games. Few rules but considered. One cormorant goes first, splashing. One page is template. A shape is apprehended, sides precise as any edge. Dissolve. Find a word before and a world after. Will the Painted Ladies rebound after the storm. Space inside definition, moving around in the house. Intensity of quiet suggests the myriad alive. A post-sunrise shadow, a post-shadow door opening. The present of participles. Beings look askance to find. Words return to the speaker, continue in a straight line forever or bounce off walls. The time of day has windows.

Drops. Rate and magnitude vary, the fact does not. Now discrete, now a texture. Hard white bon-bons the duck thought was corn. A crunchy blanket for awhile. Late intensity wavers to sleep. We might believe in this. For what is sent, get more of the same. Reaching into the wet night, listening. Send again. Clouds expect what, a reward. The river of the west. The cycle is evident. I hope I don't float away. So many circles overlapping, but only when you look. Otherwise no geometry. A very long movement, this. Where *the ephemeral is gathered by fantasy.* Pretty soon the sun comes out in China. Diminishment and pause. The fresh mingles with the salt.

Splash. After waiting unknowingly for something unexpected. This comes as no surprise. The concentricity of it. The passing from void through water to another or the same. Turns which return, as in a polygon. No signs lettered, no letters left unsigned. Read between the circumferences. What is the velocity of that. Expanding as fast as it disappears. No word on certain things, yet. If the only car ever seen on this road is a Dodge. To bark is acceptable. It soon subsides, leaving minimal damage in its wake from our perspective. Did I hyphenate correctly. This has been going on. Consider the attention it has been given. Does it have a name other than obtuse.

Snare. Staccato and roll. Enlarge the room, hit the walls. Flutter wrists to warm up, flex. Roll again into backbeat, drift and pull hard into the wind until the cadence. Wired all the while for the cue. How long you been playing kid. Try to daily. Serve it cold or hot. Invert the brass. Tell them what they're hearing and how to hear it. Begin at the level of count. Then memories and dreams of numbers. I dreamed of seeing myself double three times. You saw who? Morrison before we knew who he was. Sounds like square, but far from it. Boogie woogie from the next century. Most recent incarnation of ostinato, Densmore and Manzarek's intro riff. Then the tympani and release.

Diamond. Is enter only. On the reverse a thin coat of mercury. Quick. Tell me the names of the seven dwarves. A sliver of chance in that second movie. My brother was there to interpret the protocol. How much are jujubes. No one looked to the back and up. They say it is worth more than allowance but Saturday already exists. Campho phenique and pink tonic. Nerve medicine applied before bus and spelling test. Caught like a fly in amber. There is something you can see inside. A book on molybdenum. How do you say such a thing to your parents. A self-portrait would be very small. Its borders rhomboid. Gilt, brocade, a setting of gold.

Tar. Its implicit content. Melted and poured in a winding form. After three inches in twenty-four hours, for days the road weeps. No barrier to penetration of springs. In this case from the inside breaking out. What kind of edge cannot restrain thirty million years. Some silica in those cells. Living veins of quartz. Red List of the Silurian. Cracks in the recent lifetime. ODOT crew knows each pothole intimately. We lapse. Yes a deluge, then slick and dangerous but no one slows. Same fossil base as gas, same stink of fumes. What was under. Crossed by larval forms, indiscriminately by our standards. Orthogonally. Leaving traces and trails on the surface of a distant planet.

bridge something

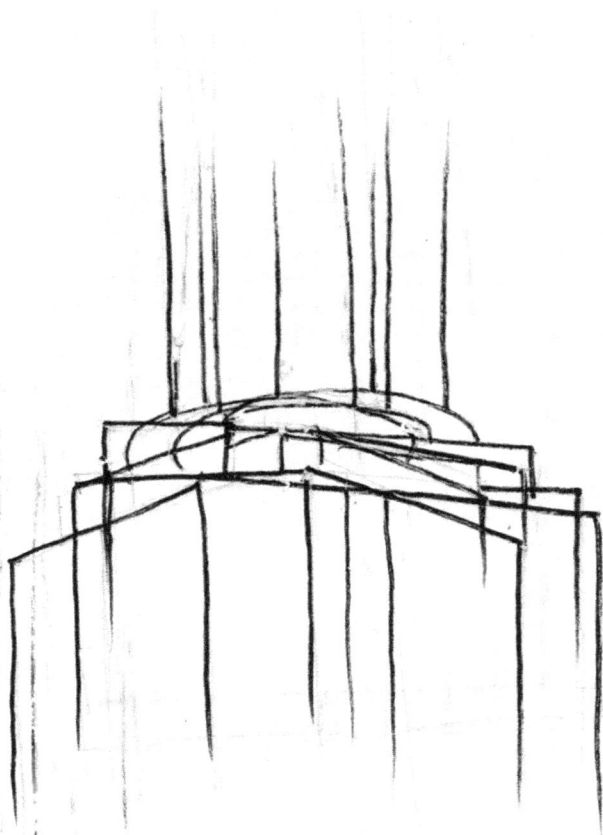

another day
in which I wandering find the subject

barn swallows in fog
see a way to move
in the wrapped world

side, side, side, side
by each, each
recognizable

played out – as a stage
constructed & left empty
long enough to realize
something has begun

this loose *while*
I write out of –
ignorant – hoping for

click –
edges almost touch –
or do –
and bridge something there

with which I have had some difficulty

which I have not always been able to see clearly

with which I have struggled for words

the names for which I have not always remembered

which has sustained me

light against, dark against

                                        its own significance

at the touch
of this to this
a meeting –

coot perched on piling inches above the river

a very long bridge connects the two states

with the hands of the eye

notes

5   Emily Dickinson (Franklin #757), 1863

13   Katagami – Japanese paper stencil patterns for textiles
         originating in the Nara Period, 710–794 – seen at Seattle
         Art Museum in 2006

18   Skokomish River and Wilderness, Southeastern Olympic
         Mountains, Washington

19   Cape Disappointment Lighthouse at the mouth of the
         Columbia River, on the Washington side

20   Parmenides, pre-Socratic philosopher of Elea –
         Unmoved and changeless in itself, [Being] stays firmly at rest,
         for strong Necessity binds and contains it by encircling limit
                             – *The Way of Truth,* c. 480 B.C.

38   (italics) Memory of a line by Cole Swenson

46   Withlacoochee River, Hernando County, Florida

53   Maurice Blanchot (on Paul Valéry), *The Writing*
         of the Disaster

54   Lake Winnemucca, north of Reno, Nevada, usually dry
         remnant of Pleistocene Lake Lahontan

54   (italics) Roland Barthes, *From Work to Text*

Art by the author:

Thanks to Bill and Matthew Yake, co-trippers through western Nevada, to Susan Darms and Roger Ley for the use of Svensen Studio, and to the support and inspiration of my wife, Christi Payne.

This book was designed by the author in the winter-into-spring rainy season, during which brant, gadwall, and snipe paid visits. It is set in Arno Pro, designed by Robert Slimbach in the tradition of early Venetian and Aldine book types.

index of genitive links

www.ingramcontent.com/pod-product-compliance
Lightning Source LLC
Chambersburg PA
CBHW032001060426
42446CB00040B/774